BASKETBALL

by Mari Schuh

AMICUS | AMICUS INK

# basket

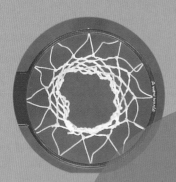

# clock

Look for these words and pictures as you read.

# lines

# uniform

Two players jump.
The game starts.
Let's watch basketball!

It is a fast game.
Each team has five
players on the court.

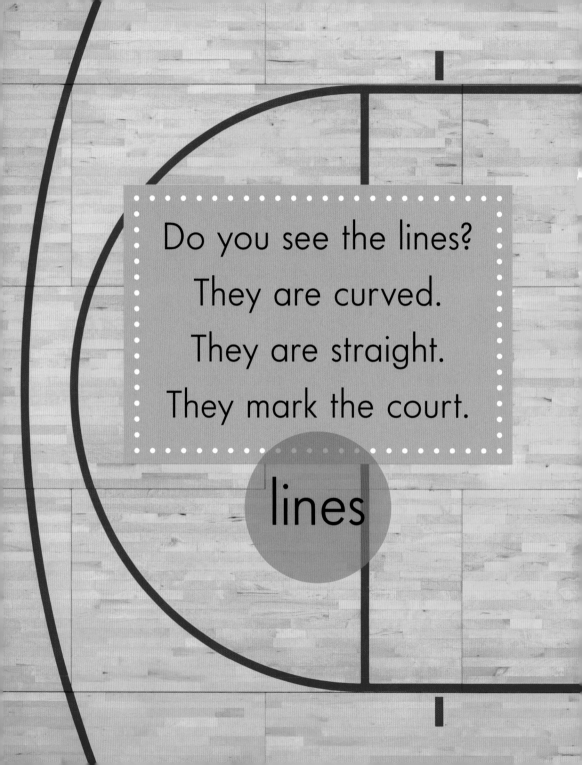

Do you see the lines?
They are curved.
They are straight.
They mark the court.

lines

# uniform

Do you see the uniform?
Each player has a number.

Do you see the basket?
A player shoots the ball.
Does it go in? Yes!
She scores two points.

basket

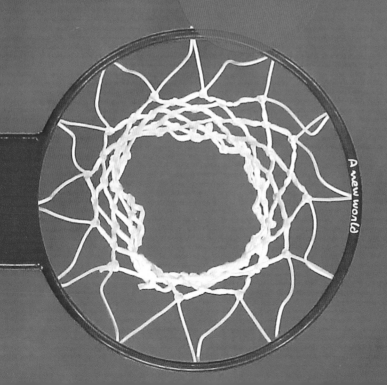

# clock

Do you see the clock?

The game will be over soon.

The crowd cheers.

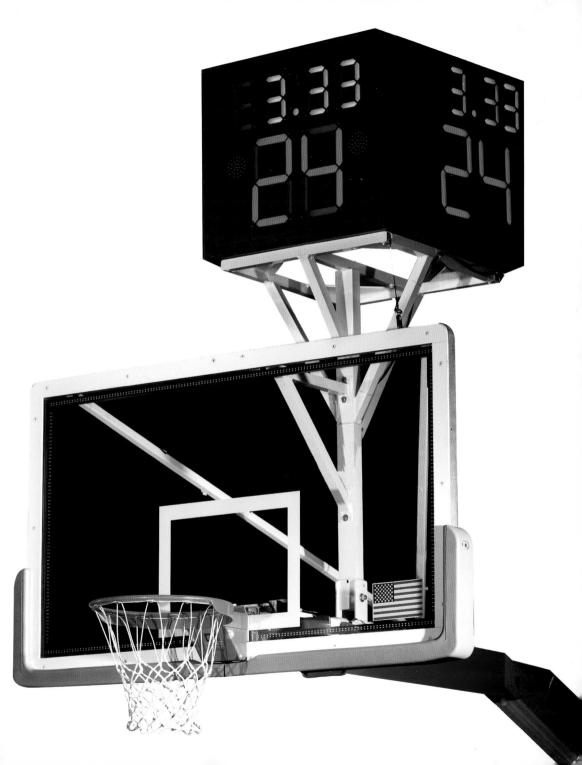

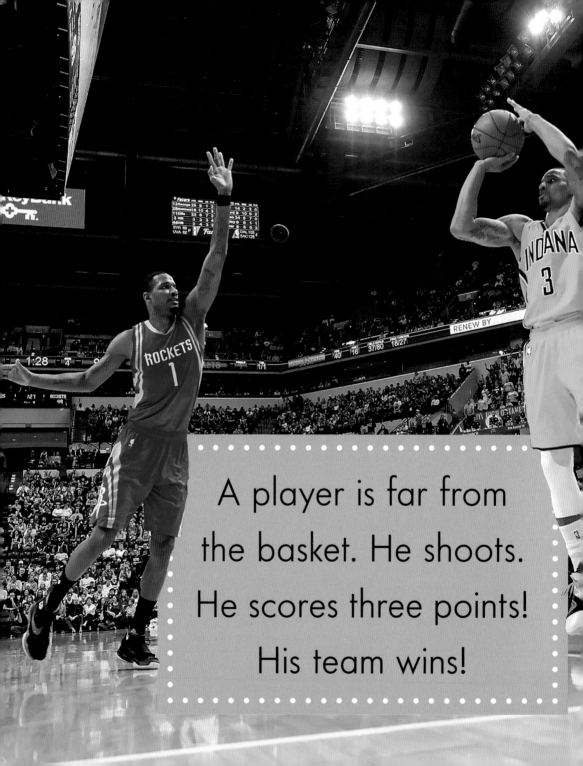

A player is far from the basket. He shoots. He scores three points! His team wins!

## basket

## clock

Did you find?

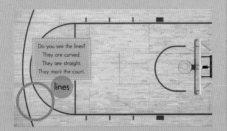

## lines

## uniform

Spot is published by Amicus and Amicus Ink
P.O. Box 1329, Mankato, MN 56002
www.amicuspublishing.us

Names: Schuh, Mari C., 1975- author.
Title: Basketball / by Mari Schuh.
Description: Mankato, Minnesota : Amicus, 2018. | Series: Spot.
  Sports | Audience: K to Grade 3.
Identifiers: LCCN 2016057195 (print) | LCCN 2016058333
  (ebook) | ISBN 9781681510842 (library binding) | ISBN
  9781681522036 (pbk.) | ISBN 9781681511740 (ebook)
Subjects: LCSH: Basketball--Juvenile literature. | Picture puzzles-
  -Juvenile literature.
Classification: LCC GV885.1 .S36 2018 (print) | LCC GV885.1
  (ebook) | DDC 796.323--dc23
LC record available at https://lccn.loc.gov/2016057195

Printed in China

HC 10 9 8 7 6 5 4 3 2 1
PB  10 9 8 7 6 5 4 3 2 1

To St. John Vianney School -- MS

Rebecca Glaser, editor
Deb Miner, series designer
Aubrey Harper, book designer
Holly Young, photo researcher

Photos by: Alamy, cover, 4–5, 8–9;
AP Photo 3, 14–15; Getty Images,
6–7, 10–11, 12–13; Shutterstock, 1

BASKETBALL